Praise for *Dear Empire*

"The poems of Holly Karapetkova do not ask for forgiveness. They willingly tackle issues of race and explore ideas associated with the anatomy of whiteness. Here is a collection that is personal as well as historical. Karapetkova writes with a contagious honesty. Her poems describe an American mirror we should not turn away from. Karapetkova's biblical references are a reminder that there is always goodness at the center of her work."

> —E. Ethelbert Miller, writer and literary activist
> 2024 Grammy Nominee for Spoken Word and Poetry

"For the moments, months, and centuries when we don't know our own faces, these poems might be a cure. *Dear Empire* is a mirror we desperately need. These poems show us histories and violence some choose not to see. This mirror shows us George Washington's true face, it shows us a train carrying migrants fleeing violence, it shows us history we erased, the lynched humans we documented on postcards. This mirror warns us, with biblical seriousness, that not seeing creates more than blindness. It allows a lie. Holly Karapetkova's poems help us ask questions, they make us brave, they invite us to see. Do not look away from the beauty and power in these poems."

> —Joseph Ross, author of *Raising King* and *Crushed & Crowned*

"If the story of America were a Bible, a testament of creation, exile, rules for life, and acculturation, and if, instead of parables and origin stories, it told the history of lynchings and genocides, but from the point of view of the white bystander, you would eventually come to this—it would inevitably be this book—*Dear Empire*—translated, in effect, by a poet, into the language of poetry, and using as its prophets James Baldwin and Ta-Nehesi Coates. Behind all of this, Holly Karapetkova has written a tour de force: a tender but deeply candid volume which seeks to de-colonize not the country but the self, stripping off the sticky layers of old personal debts and regrets, our fairy tales and illusions, the ghosts of our idols, and our historical atrocities, until what is left is "the space/ between the spaces" where an opening silence and not unproductive emptiness shows us finally where and what are. *Dear Empire* aims to alchemize the emptiness; it does so with brilliant self-compassion and deft understanding in the end. "Genesis," "Exodus," "High Hat," "Rapunzel," "Dear White" and "The Book of the American Republic" are masterful works, as are so many other poems in this unforgettable collection."

—David Keplinger, author of *Ice: Poems*

"In *Dear Empire*, it is history that Holly Karapetkova addresses—and would have us address. History is a cabinet in a great room filled with mirrors and relics, some made "of ivory, cow teeth, slave teeth." It is thus the story of slavery, lynching, cyclical dispossessions. And history is the story of what happened, regardless of who was or wasn't there, as told by those with the *power* to circulate narratives. If only we could see clear through each other, the poet writes. But as her deft and incisive poems show, history is also the story of survival, sacrifice, and devotion; of how we are always running toward that light which can't be bought or stolen."

—Luisa A. Igloria, author *Caulbearer* and *Maps for Migrants and Ghosts*

"In *Dear Empire* poet Holly Karapetkova offers a serious, ambitious excavation of White witness. In "Dear White" she writes, "You are the last lie/the lover/I can't shake free./... I moan your name in my sleep." Karapetkova fearlessly scrutinizes her own complicity, undertaking an emotional inventory of the insidiousness of White supremacy and its coupling with White femininity. These poems are lyrical prescriptions, the necessary conversation that some avoid over family holidays, their stunning truths—a smoking indictment of a culture and country long overdue for a reckoning."

—Teri Ellen Cross Davis, author of *a more perfect Union* and *Haint*

Dear Empire

Published by Gunpowder Press
Edited by David Starkey and Chryss Yost
PO Box 60035
Santa Barbara, CA 93160-0035

Front cover image: Photo by Herbert Tonkin, "Alice and Gertie Guthrie
25 & De Haro Sts. / / Tonkin, 1227 Market St., San Francisco, Cal."
c. 1900. From Library of Congress Prints and Photographs Division.
https://www.loc.gov/pictures/item/2016650203/

ISBN-13: 978-1-957062-20-4

Library of Congress Control Number: 2024926560

www.gunpowderpress.com

Gunpowder Press is part of Gunpowder Poetry, a 501(c)(3) nonprofit
literary organization. The Barry Spacks Poetry Prize is supported in
part by the Santa Barbara Poetry Fund under the auspices of the Santa
Barbara Foundation.

Dear Empire

Poems

Holly Karapetkova

Gunpowder Press • Santa Barbara
2025

For my parents,
my first and best teachers,
who read me my first poems.

Contents

I

II

I

Genesis

Like any mother I lived for my children. Bone of my bones, gave them my body as house, gave them my house as home. I was fruitful, I multiplied. Nothing was ever my own and I called this sacrifice, devotion. What I called them became their names. Some grew and some did not. Some were angry and some were not. Some murdered, some tended the flocks, some built boats to escape the flood. Some built towers into the sky. Some became pillars of salt. I fed them by the sweat of my brow. Some needed more than I could give them, though I saved only thorns and thistles for myself. God was a voice in the sky with no tree to burn. God was a shower of sulfur, a snake winding through the dirt. If I had a moment to spare, I might have bent to hear what he was saying.

Bad Parenting

Out back smoking a cigarette
below the window where no one can find me.

The children are calling *mommy! where are you!*
but when are they not asking for me?

In the cold my breath rises like smoke
even when I don't take a drag.

The children are beginning to worry.
The seven-year-old yells louder.

The two-year-old starts to cry.
It's only a matter of minutes before they think

to look for me here, but I need every minute
I can get to figure out what happened to my life,

sort through the details of this accident—
the fur still lodged in white bumper paint

and the sound of muscle meeting metal
then dashing off into the night.

Spotting the Whale

I have lived where whales live—
off the southern tip of an island,
just beyond the shore of a peninsula.

I have taken boats far on the water,
stared hours into the sunset,
waves rippling out before me
gentle as a furrowed field
or large enough to knock a fishing boat under

and never have I seen a whale, not one
round roll of a head, not a single
spout blowing saltwater into the air.

My eyes follow every white patch
in the current, every black break
in a ripple—always just a trick of shadow,
a large fish too close to sunlight.

Whale, someone shouts
from the other side of the ship—
but by the time I reach the stern
it has disappeared.

You'll say I don't know
what I'm looking for
though I have watched a hundred films
read every book with the name

still unable to spot what swims beside me,
beneath me, so close I could call it
familiar.

Neighborhood Games

They arrived on long yellow buses
from neighborhoods across town,

the long list repeated daily in homeroom:
Schwanna, Demont, Tayara, Valencia,

names we never used. They sat
at their own lunch table, formed

their own game of tag at recess.
We were German-Polish-Norwegian-Italian-

Scottish-British-*white*, the unwritten rules
we'd already learned by heart.

At home we ran the neighborhood,
played capture the flag, tackle football,

snowball wars, ally ally in come free.
A wilderness grew behind our houses,

acres and acres untamed. We made
a secret hideout, dug a hole that could hold

several of us at a time. I remember
the view from inside, earth reaching

to my shoulders, a hole so deep
we had to climb down in it to keep digging.

W[h]it[e]ness

No one had to say the word

                white

what it meant

                clear

as the air in my lungs

                breathe

clear as nothing is clear

                look

No one had to sit me

                down

in the kitchen

                say

your eyes

                your hair

my body

                light

a window

                you could

see right

                through

We Are the World

United Support of Africa, 1985

We sang for the starving black kids
in Africa we'd never meet

avoided the black kids
we saw every day at school

in the stairwell
in the bathroom

where we'd belt out
  change can only come

off key *pretending day by day*
wanting to grow up wanting

  the truth, you know
echoing off the brown tiles

and frosted window glass
back into our own ears.

We thought we sounded
so good thought

  love is all we need
we could save the world without

  a choice we're making
staring back at our own

faces in the mirror
  just you and me.

Big Hair

We all wanted it, endured hours in the salon chair:
hair wrapped around hard plastic rollers,

chemicals dripping on our scalps.
Then each morning the curling iron,

clouds of chlorofluorocarbons, hair spray
coating every surface of the bathroom.

We didn't know (didn't ask) that the black girls
were doing the same thing in the opposite direction,

relaxers and straightening irons to pull out
the curls they didn't want, get something

approaching the texture of white hair.
In the yearbook we're all smiling,

white girls with bangs puffed like carnations,
black girls with hair sculpted into orchids,

our pictures alphabetical, interspersed
so you'd think we were friends,

could turn to one another in homeroom one morning
and complain about the rain ruining

45 minutes of hair preparation. But we didn't.
We suffered at separate ends of the yard,

monkey bars and playground dust rising between,
a distance none of us could imagine crossing.

"Was He Good to His Slaves?"

On a tour at Mount Vernon

The question hangs in the air of the New Room
        by the mirror on the wall.

      The guide has heard it before
           like cherry trees and wooden teeth.
    He explains the acts of resistance
          and attempts at escape
             without missing a beat.

The tall looking glass, however, is original
          and was purchased
    from a French envoy's estate.

    We watch ourselves walk past it
      as (we are told)
Washington must have watched himself dancing
         centuries ago.

      I imagine his reflection
         father of a nation
        mouth closed to hide his teeth
   which were made not of wood
         but of ivory, cow teeth, slave teeth.

The teeth were paid for.
      The slaves were paid for,
         property passed down
   with all of its issue and increase.

Out on the lawn the sun is setting
      low on the horizon.
  We squint our eyes against the light
 shining us straight in the face.

   It's impossible to see ahead
though anyone coming from the other direction
  must see us clearly
      all our colors lit.

High Hat

The man on the horse has the high ground, the high air, the high hat. He moves as fast as (if not the wind) a beast, having claimed a beast and made it ride. He claims the ground, arriving first to stick in his flag. The man on the horse looks down at you when he talks. His words fall, heavy as clods of dirt off the side of a cliff, which makes you think of avalanche, all that earth unmoored. The man on the horse asks no questions, wants no answers from another's mouth. He sees the sun set a few seconds before you and so claims the setting. He claims you, too, in a manner, since you must work for someone. You with your two feet on the ground, not fast enough to arrive anywhere first. Get used to the sky shot open, the sound of birds searching for a place to rest. Look as far as you can: you own nothing in sight.

We Thought We Were

"Americans believe in the reality of 'race' as a defined, indubitable feature of the natural world."

—Ta-Nehisi Coates

Mouthwash in the medicine cabinet
        toilet paper quilted
quiet on the streets after dark
        crickets the only sound
combing the block
        the blades of their legs sharp
our straight straight hair
        combed straight down our backs
or pinioned into pigtails
        nothing piggish about us
our pink pink skin
        paper cuts
staunched with gauze
        two cars in every garage
garbage placed on the curb
        we kept our hands clean
upper crust
        cream of the crop
we were seasons siphoned off
        & sipped through a straw:
a held breath.
        Natural law.

Breakfast of Champions

I am awakened each morning
by a million pixels:

the light of my own face,
selfie smiling on my smartphone.

I breathe in the air of 14.5 planets,
breathe out 20 metric tons of carbon

before I even brush my teeth.
My gold medal is bigger than yours

and it's got nothing to do with luck;
it's all pluck and hard work

and tax breaks targeted
to stimulate the economy,

this stamina I acquired
by pushing my checkbook

from one bank to the next
in search of lower interest rates.

They fall like stars into my hat
and thanks to my elite

education I've learned
to stuff them in my pockets,

thousands of points of light,
to touch them until they respond

with the image I want to see.
They shine every morning, only for me.

Klepto

If you want to hang onto your wallet you shouldn't be drinking vodka. If you want starlight in a bottle don't look at me. I have my own shirts to iron and if I'd wanted your money I would've taken it. Likewise your advice, shadows on a social media train of thought, slow pan downward to the square where the smiling family waits. There's always a smiling family, or a sad dog looking up at you. Have you learned nothing from your MBA in marketing? I have a degree in thin air. I make up the rules as I go along, find a just cause and paste it on my website. No need to look offended— the beautiful are always beautiful and the damned are always damned. You just have to figure out which one is which.

Winner Takes All

Because there aren't enough spots
on the dice for you to win fair

and square every time.
Because when you count

your money into little
piles at night you always see

double. Because from up
on this cliff you can't tell

whether the bodies
in the lake below are swimming

or drowning. From up here
your rambler feels more

like a castle, draw bridge slammed
shut, a book no one needs

to read to know the end of.
Where there's a front door there's a right

of refusal, a bell to make
a statement: this house only has one

story and you're
going to be the one telling it.

Dear Empire

Blue-eyed wonder of the universe,
you have all the answers.

If you stopped breathing
the world would wheeze to a stop—

milky way run out of milk,
solar system spit out its moons,

rivers stop running bereft
of so many bodies.

No one can wreck
without your wrecking ball,

shoot without your 6-gauge,
piss without your chamber pot.

Though you paid fair market value
this land is not yours.

Though its denizens break
their backs for your paltry wage

their minds are running
toward their own horizon

where the sun rises,
a light you can't steal.

II

Exodus

I've lived long enough to know that when locusts arrive they are always a plague; the red sea is always full of reeds. When the war came to the village of god, I cannot say it caught me by surprise, though I was not prepared for the ash falling, breaking our skin into boils. I gathered my children and ran, the older ones carrying the younger, the youngest carrying what they could. The desert swam before us like a chasm of needs, an empty scroll, the unsewn hem of a nation. When the food ran out we begged, when there was nothing to beg we starved. No manna appeared, no flock of quail. We left the lame behind to save the strong, knowing there were hungrier beasts following in our wake. The lambs. This was god's lesson to us on the journey out: not everyone survives.

Social Studies

In 5th grade we learned
that slavery ended in 1865:
thirteenth amendment

(turn the page)

Indian Removal Act in 1830
Trail of Tears 1838-1839
meant for their own protection (sic)

(end of chapter)

This is what makes us social
these studies
a long list of presidents

(cotton plantation on this very playground)

wars whose dates we memorize
treaties and purchases

(just the facts)

the Mason Dixon Line
thickened on the map
reservations shaded blue as sky

(Cherokee genocide just north of here)

a fugitive pencil crossing

(erase)

Callaway Went Thataway (1951)

This picture was made in the spirit of fun, and was meant in no way to detract from the wholesome influence, civic mindedness and the many charitable contributions of Western idols of our American youth, or to be a portrayal of any of them.
                    —Film Disclaimer

                    Made in the spirit of fun:
                              an Injun
down the barrel of a wide-angle lens—

                         the forces of evil
                                        gripping their tomahawks.

    It's not genocide it's self defense
              this picture—

a portrayal of our American youth
                         wholesome

          with many charitable contributions
                              civic and civic minded
                    Western as a setting sun
                         come to barter

                    a mouthful of lead
                              a wagon full of trinkets

                         in the spirit of fun
this picture
                    was made for.

In the Past, the Present Is the Future

And Paul Newman is younger than you are now, his sideways glance and twitchy smile harder to resist than your look of pity, fake a frown. He was faking, too, of course, but so convincingly I took it for fact, in the past, when the past was the present or at least more present than it is now. You were waiting out in the future, your face still full of promise, nothing yet tangible, nothing yet filled in with bone. You slipped from your saddle and I stooped to pick you up, but that was the future and the future was ahead. The present was Paul Newman in his reckless jeans, though as Butch Cassidy he was already beginning to show some tufts of gray. The past was catching up to him, the saying goes, as my past is catching up to you now, and you won't see it coming until the present is miles behind you and the future is just another man on a horse a few gallops up ahead.

La Bestia

As many as half a million Central American immigrants annually hop aboard freight trains colloquially known as "La Bestia," or the beast, on their journey to the United States.
　　　　　　—Rodrigo Dominguez Villegas, *Migration Policy Institute*

On its back they are coming

San Pedro Sula
San Salvador

　　tracks split like a cracked jaw
Guatemala
Distrito Central
　　　　　　chokepoint

La Bestia ripping the night open

　　2000 miles
　　fever and rust

　　　　a thousand, a hundred thousand
coming

　　to mow our lawns
　　clean our houses

Sasabe and San Luis
Santa Teresa
　　spit out into the desert

they are coming

        to install our cabinets
        our marble floors

the imprint of their careful fingers
around each cartoned strawberry

            we send them back and still
            they come
        to scrub out the toilets

we will soil and flush
soil
        and flush again

There Are Boats

There are boats
and people sail them
out to sea
out past the sight of land
across an ocean
full of sharks.

There are boats
and people on them
far out at sea
deep in the pockets
of a gathering storm.

There are boats
that sink
and boats that float
boats made of
metal and wood
and boats made
of inflatable plastic

full of children
full of mothers
floating with nothing
but what they could carry
carrying nothing
but the air beneath them.

Still Sea

Sea unseen is
what the I sees
where
a window
is flinging open

Still sea
does not determine
the shores end
A wave
against the rocks

Where the I enters
an ankle
cups itself in
a hand
or being held
aloft
gently

The water parts for
an elbow
the palm of
a holding
the body
rising
on a wave

The same sea that rips
grain from grain
mounts
the last resort
closing on a wave

Mountain to sand
a wall of water
drowning the city
the sun's eye
far from shore

Where the I enters
it takes hold and
it will carry

The water shifts
what it holds
beyond seeing

Wrack

The ocean doesn't ask forgiveness.
Overnight in a sudden fit of disgust
it thrusts mound upon mound of seaweed
on the shore, the pale sand a tangle
of mahogany and rust for half a kilometer.
Then slowly over several months,
one high tide at a time, it takes
each lamina back as though it had forgotten
the story it was reading and why,
its long arm arching over the words
and filling them with its own music
rushing toward us in a loud hush—
as though it could ask for silence.

Lynching: A Brief History

Start with a river.
Let it be deep and wide.
Let it pass 10,000 cubic feet
of water per second.
There are still things that won't
sink, that won't be washed
to sea.
        Start with what floats.
Start with what snags a log,
circles back in an eddy.
Start with a word, a whistle,
even a look will do.
Start with the source:
a trickle down a steep cliff
gathering breath.
And what is washed away
will not be made clean.

Southern Gothic

Sometimes the moss in a tree
is just moss.

Sometimes it is a body
swinging from a rope.

How you tell the difference
is by getting close enough to see,

by waiting for the sun to rise
high enough to clear off

the shadows stuck
to your own feet.

The boy was just a boy,
not a big-eyed monster.

The river was cold and the wind
colder. This is how it works:

I hit you and you scream.
This is how it plays out:

I wring you like a dishcloth
and the truth gushes forth—

the only truth
that will make it out of here alive.

Dear White

For decades
I've borrowed
your clothes
without asking,
inserted
your address
on job applications,
taken the birthday
money and never
written a thank-you.

I've played phone tag
with identity politics,
planted *seeds*
of change in gardens
where nothing grew;
I kept them
free of weeds.

You are the last lie,
the lover
I can't shake free.
I tell myself
I've moved on now.
I moan your name
in my sleep.

History

is not where you left it
up on the mantel
in a silver frame

or at the bottom of the trunk
mildewing in the basement.

Outside a dog is barking
and you have no idea why.

Outside a kid is screaming—
it sounds like your kid

but then you remember
your kid is a grown man now.

Inside the clothes are ironed,
the shelves dusted,
and still some small thought escapes:

a curtain stained
like a black eye.

Come on over, you call
out the window
to no one in particular.

Come on over,
and no one will.

Generosity

The late dictator was a generous man, given to torture only on Sundays and only after offering his subjects a choice among several artistically choreographed positions. He had once been a poet of questionable talent, and while no one dared to recall the quality of his verses, his pen name had taken up most of the cover space on his books and was difficult to forget.

Like the worst Roman Emperors, the dictator was extremely popular during his early years in office; all of the children born in the first decade of the regime were given one of his names in tribute. Later, it was said he derived great pleasure from calling his victims by their names, his own names, during the torture process. It seemed at moments when the pain set in that he was both giver and receiver, victim and tormentor, until he could no longer tell the other's body from his own, his life from another's death. The pain expanded out before him like an open sea. He dove down so deep no name could call him out.

III

Leviticus

A woman who gives birth is unclean, and all flying insects that walk on four legs. I wanted order, cleanliness, a place to walk without stepping on something hard and hurtful, stones piled in the corner. I started making rules. I hung them on the walls like scrolls, the book that no one reads: No running in the house. Pick up after yourself. Leave your dirt at the entrance, scrape your dishes clean. Nothing extraordinary. The plan was sanity, clarity. Instead I spent my breath yelling *dirty hands off the manna*. I wound myself up like a top and set myself spinning. How many animals in a herd, a flock, how many doves torn open by the wings, crushed heads of the new grain: a burnt offering, a sin offering, a guilt offering. Take scarlet yarn and hyssop. Take the stones, timbers and all the plaster. Take the live bird from an open field. A message from a voice somewhere on fire.

Phantoms

After Lord Nelson lost his right arm during an unsuccessful attack on Santa Cruz de Tenerife, he experienced compelling phantom limb pains [... which] led the sea lord to proclaim that his phantom was "direct proof of the existence of the soul." If an arm can survive physical annihilation, why not the entire person?

—V. S. Ramachandran

If an arm why not a person
             if a person why not a soul
    if a soul why not god
             if god why not my children

the ones with their heads
    curled against their chests
          furled fronds of a fern
     heads a bulge a node
that never opens

why not let them grow
      on their own now
    that they have left me
           the entire person
      why not a limb   a lobe

why not let them kick
     their stub toes   almost elbows
  let them grow stronger
       while my breasts sag
    back against my chest

let them spin and spin
        themselves into being
their stories   those small engines
              tight threads curled
              around my finger
      waiting for a name.

Zombies

My son is afraid of zombies. He runs into my room at night. *They're going to eat my brains! They'll come in through the windows while we're sleeping and eat our brains!*

Don't worry, I tell him, zombies don't exist. *But what if they do?* They don't. *But maybe they do.* They don't. *But maybe they do.*

We walk through the house together, checking each door and window; everything's latched tight. See, I tell him, no way zombies could get in. He's not convinced. I dig out the water we brought back from the sacred spring, where pilgrims wait in line to be healed. I sprinkle it on his head, make crosses on his wrists. He's satisfied and falls asleep.

I stay awake, hear insects scraping their wings against the windows, leaves shifting beneath the empty sky. I spread the sacred water by each window, each doorstep, watching. What is there in the darkness is always looking in, dead-eyed and hankering for flesh. I watch it walk, arms raised, almost human.

Without Sanctuary

Photographs and Postcards of Lynching in America

I turn to leave
but it is always sunset.

The shadows stretch,
each knuckle a knot,

each tree a body
shifting in the wind.

In the postcard photograph
white faces crowd in to watch;

I cannot see their features
clearly enough to know

I am not among them.
On the back a photo credit,

a county and state, proof
of witness.

Sometimes a note.
Coon cooking.

*All OK and would like
to get a post from you.*

Then a scrawled signature,
a name and address:

Strike a match,
we all go up in smoke.

Gunpowder Logic

Give me periwigs and high boots.
Give me a New World
and call it Virgin,
the promise of someone else's body
torn up at the roots:
cash crops,
forests jackknifed open
and payment shackled at the ankles.

Give me wood from a tree
hewn to a plank,
a space I leave blank
dragged through salt and storm
across the length of an ocean
and dumped here at my feet
ready to be called whatever
I name it in my language.

I Was Born

with sunscreen
smeared across my legs,
arms so white
they smelled like marshmallow cream.

I was so pale
the teacher sent me home
sick every day.

No, my mother told her
when she came to pick me up,
she's just white.

When I stand at the white wall
you see nothing
but my eyes.

When I stand against the sky
you think I'm clouds
and maybe I am—

so full of nothing I float
clear into the blue.

Even the Space

Can I say one word
that isn't white—
                  the space
      around the words
                      the silence
          behind every door

        the inside of my mouth
            my ribcage
light hitting the sidewalk
                  bouncing back

into nothing
            fields and fields of light
      all colors faded bleached
                a ghost

                howling in the margin
      which I left white   completely

a mirror I can see into but not out of
          a mirror that   no matter
   what I throw at it
            refuses to break.

Power: A Brief History

I was born
with my finger
in the socket, hair so
white they called me
lightning: nothing
could turn me off. I

have forces no
one understands, can spark
a chainsaw with my bare
hands, set
the town on fire
by speaking
in tongues. When

you walk the streets
my hot breath swells
behind you;
when you sleep
at night I watch
with lidless eyes.

There's no word
you can whisper
that I won't simmer
to a vapor,

no flag you can wave
that isn't already flaming
against my sky.

The Invisible Man (1933)

Don't worry—I was never really here, the knot of laughing gas, the matrix I entered and entered until I reached the blank page where my nose should've been. All it took was a mixture of the right chemicals, the right proportions, and the blank page waiting to break the bonds that tied me to myself. Fill it with truths that fit in my hands: A hot mess of wishful thinking will drive the prices up. Pour a glass of champagne, pop the bubble of discontent.

See how my *freedom* blooms violently to fill the empty space: the wrong man made right, the rapist was just fooling around, this 70 degree December was what we expected all along. Nothing a little cold cash can't settle. The map that shows the temperatures rising is so red it burns my fingers.

You choose your facts and I'll choose mine. Unwrap the bandages from my head: there's nothing there.

Dear America

I called and no one answered.
I left voice messages,

sent texts and emails
lost in the ether.

Tell me things aren't
as bad as they seem.

Tell me that's not
a bullwhip in your back pocket,

smallpox on your hands,
fossil fuels foaming

between your teeth.
Tell me when *la migra*

pounds on the door,
when blue lights flash

beneath an overpass
and drones swarm the sky

like birds of prey
they leave no bodies behind.

Tell me only the map
is darkening,

only the sun passing
behind a cloud.

IV

Numbers

The mother is always to blame: 40 years in the wilderness, count the decades on one hand. I am in my 40th year and life is a wilderness of children. I cannot count them all. The census lists the sons of the tribe. No one lists the daughters. The daughters list anxiety, depression, paranoia, phobia. They grow like the hairs on my head, heading for a world in which a woman is always to blame, sinking like a stone in the river of god. The test for an unfaithful wife is dust in holy water, the bitter water that brings a curse; if she then bears no child she has not sinned. I bear children, a long list of offerings, a long list of deserts. I spent decades following a husband who was following a cloud. I would like to speak with you alone, but this is impossible. I wander into rivers hoping to find solace or solitude. A door slams and I remember where I am: a desert. There is no water and someone will be blamed.

Still Life

I always wanted to be
a good girl, white
as a canvas,
a knuckled grip.

This meant holding
my breath.
This meant
counting to ten

or ten thousand,
watching
all the lights
in the city

for something
to flicker:
a secret message,
a passage out.

Nothing ever appeared
but a distant flash
of lightning,
roadside sign

with its mouth
full of neon
blinking
XXX

silence,
the shadows of white
roses darkening the sidewalk.

White Magic

Pixie dust on the floor
of the NYSE:

I was taught
to marry for money.

Send me a fairy godmother
when my credit's maxed.

Slip me the glass slipper
when no one's looking

and charge it
to the footman.

Take me to the ball
and back

in my Armani Privé gown
before anything strikes.

The pumpkin is always
just a pumpkin.

My hands
are covered in soot.

Rapunzel

To the tall tower I went willingly: No door meant no key, nothing to open but a window high above the trees. The birds landed on the sill singing; I held them in my hands and twisted until their heads came free, a mess of feathers at my feet. They kept coming, the birds, the men with their faces soft as feathers. They climbed up through my window and told me I was fair as sunlight—what was such a creature doing alone in these woods? I let them twitter on and on, the witch a story I told to lull them to sleep. The knots of my hair coiled about the sheets, but they never saw it coming. The men were always blinded. My hair was short as a thicket of thorns.

Rage

When you turned and left
    something turned in me:
             a knot
      a ringing
           ripping through me
like a key's
      cold metal.

      I held it in my mouth
    as I could not hold you

      the jagged edge
scraping my tongue.

It tasted nothing
            like you
    so bitter
I lived on it for days
though it fed me nothing

       it fit
    so perfectly

and the door it opened
      was far bigger
then me   far bigger
    than the both of us

      and I went through.

Four and Twenty

I baked 24 blackbirds in a pie and when I cut it open the sound of their voices filled the room. After that I figured anything could happen. After that I was not easily surprised. There was a counting house and a king with money, there was a queen distracted by bread and honey, I had sixpence and a small sack of rye. I was young and pretty. I did things with my body. I cut myself into 24 bird-sized bites and fed myself to the king. When I was opened a great singing commenced. It was the sound of his money falling into my mouth and the great chasm of the sky spitting out birds like bad seeds. They snipped and snipped until not a single nose was left, the clothes swinging from the line like a thousand emptied souls, their bodies snipped clean into nothing. I was not surprised. I was never hungry. I sang for my supper.

Dowry Song

Eggshell is the name of a color
debt up to the eyeballs:
as much as a car
who says
white
on a white picket fence
how many
snipped at the stem
the rain comes hard
don't wish for the obvious
I never wanted to live here
all that water
the jug
tied to the tree root
the knives
give me a nickel after midnight
give me white dander

cocaine sugar
that dress cost
a pretty penny
money isn't
moth wing
pretty but
hundreds of roses
to cover the altar
don't wish for the flood
the blank check
I wanted the house by the river
rushing past
cold whiskey
dress deflating
in the spoon rack
I know where to spend it
on a white white rose

Dear White Girl

Dear errata. Apology. Dear sugar and spice, cherry and cherry pop. Dear pillar of salt, pillar of the plantation, love and charity to all. Dear Barbie doll in a permanent ball gown, Barbie Dream House and who'd she have to marry to end up there. Dear laurel tree and hollow reeds. Dear sorrow-become-stone, caged-in-the-forest, turned-into-a-bird. Dear picked flowers, wild and domesticated. Dear Wyoming and Louisiana and 81 cents to the dollar. Dear Scylla and Charybdis, Good Witches of the North and South, Governor's wife, Overseer's wife, CEO's wife, slumlord's wife. I didn't mean what I said. Please don't let me end up with that old maid card in my hand.

Snow White

Once it was thought the sun made people black,
that removed from Africa, skin
would gradually lighten into winter—
not to be confused with the real change
that took place as slave masters
raped women and raped them again:
quadroon, octaroon, quintroon, tell me who
is the fairest. The mirror stares back
like the hunter's gun. What all women want:
to walk out into the snow and disappear.

The Pea

Believe me no true princess would go wandering around lost in the woods alone—unless she were taken there by the queen's huntsman and left for the wolves to finish off. No true princess would beg at a stranger's door, sleep on a stranger's bed piled with mattresses to the ceiling, unless—

Believe me, this is not a happy story.

As for the pea, the prick of the spindle, how they force their way into the deepest sleep, the most secret chambers of the castle. Even the richest and most coddled of us eventually finds herself sleeping in a stranger's bed, lost in a stranger's wood.

Pretend it's a pea if you like; call it round, green, and wholesome. It still won't let you sleep.

Fragments Reconstructed from a Poem

(From Sappho, trans. Willis Barnstone)

embroidered   my pain drips
    behind a laurel tree the loom   disarms

desire   poured
        salt sea

        mortal women   awake

your face   a deed   I am coming
your face   a lyre   I want

    riverbanks   wreaths
          tongues   oil

remind   us Eros
      you burn   whiter than an egg

floating   my voice is empty

    swollen   iron knives
      dim corpses   tender breasts

basket and oar
    embroidered   my pain drips
      I am coming

The Life of Objects

My body
is a boat
fastened with rope
where water
trips on the skirt
of its tide.
One man built me
another man bought me
& so I wait
nailed & tied
to carry him across.

What I want
is to untether
to row myself
out to open ocean
be torn apart
& there
to float
driftwood
drunk with salt,
to wash ashore
on a nameless island
where no one
& nothing
says mine.

The Rest of Her

She left her little finger behind when she rushed out the door. We tried to call her back but she was gone and there it sat, pink as you please on the dressing table. We were sure it would unlock something—we searched the house from attic to basement, crammed its nail into every trunk and drawer lock and still couldn't find what to open. Instead, we divided it into joints and each wore one like an amulet. Cut the hoodoo, said our neighbors, but we needed all the luck we could get, and point made six months later when she was found noosed with a telephone cord and hanging from a stairwell. It was then we realized we should have taken more while we had the chance—a leg, a lip, a handful of hair. Now she was gone for good and the rest of her would be of no use to anyone.

Photo Negative

Experience is
more than
my sunburn, is
a thousand different shapes
of a single wave,
shapes which are not
the point of
the motion
opening
the old wound—
it also burns;
I have seen
shapes of
your face
each of them
shadows rising—
should I leave?

Would my going tell you
who you are, or simply
what will not stay still
down the shore, dissolving
leaving unanswered
the sea—
is it physics,
chemistry,
the coldness
rising around a calf,
algae, wave, sand,
ship:

Not truth, not
the cold wet sting of
the sea. I could see
in the foam
if only it would stay put,
the sea, not
the water's motion
reaching
the door—
salt water heals but
what to do now
a thousand different
sufferings pass
knowing I have caused
in turn
the thousand and first—
should I stay?

What is the truth of who I am,
of the wave,
its foam sliding back
into the current,
the true nature of
how to define it—
an angle of motion,
a bond between atoms
circling an ankle—
is it salt, water,
is it fish, dolphin,
of course it is

none of
our minds empty
with the shore,
the wind and water carving
a space,
but does it matter
in the current

these but
place us here
with the sound of
rock. You loved me
true,
now you are
moving away.

There Is Only Now

"We are told to accept what is happening to us because of ancestors wrong doing, but it is all based on historical lies..."
—From the journal of the white supremacist who killed nine African Americans during a Bible study at Emanuel African Methodist Episcopal Church in Charleston, South Carolina

Nothing happened.
I was there.
I was not there.
The body swung
like a pitchfork. The bodies
hung like lanterns from
the bridge. Their mouths
were stuffed
with rags.

This never happened.
This still happens
every time I cross
the bridge, black
bodies swaying
above the water, white
bodies crowding
on the bridge looking
down to see.

Am I more
afraid of a corpse or my
shadow, my shadow
or my hands, the blind

spot, the rope
pulling and those white
bodies looking down:

their faces
blurred against
the background
like ghosts.

"The Book of the American Republic"
—James Baldwin

Chapter 1:

Nothing is written
One must assume...

If one has hands wear white gloves

leave no prints

pages smooth   a blank check

mouth empty   faced

If one must ride the bus   the subway

clutch one's purse   one's jaw tight

Say nothing

Chapter 2:

A long sigh seething between the pages

Exasperation, one might call it

the smack of a spotlight in the face

father of the races

one must be patient

give charity   where charity is earned
          a tithe   a pain divided into lashes

Repeat it until you mean it
                    then turn to the previous page

Chapter 3:

          Open at the middle
and begin again

          Head bonneted hands
                    avoid work   avoid sun

     pages whitening   into pages
                    a blank   stare

          Someone else will clean the carpet   the shoes

     the space between   the spaces

the instructions rising to greet you

          eeny meeny miny mo   on every continent

the song learns
                    to sing itself

ACKNOWLEDGEMENTS

Grateful acknowledgement is made to the publications in which the following poems first appeared:

Alaska Quarterly Review: "Lynching: A Brief History" (published as "Lynchburg"), "I Was Born" (Published as "Dear White"), and "Dear Empire" (Published as "Dear White")

Arlington Literary Journal: "Social Studies" and "Neighborhood Games"

Barrelhouse online: "Zombies" and "The Invisible Man"

Bennington Review: "High Hat" and "Klepto"

Blackbird: "Fragments Reconstructed from a Poem" and "There are Boats"

Blue Earth Review: "Exodus" and "Numbers" ("Numbers" also appeared in *Best Short Fiction* 2020)

Clockhouse: "La Bestia"

Cortland Review: "The Life of Objects"

Crab Orchard Review: "Breakfast of Champions"

Delmarva Review: "Winner Takes All"

Descant: "The Book of the American Republic" (as "White Manual")

ellipsis... literature & art: "Callaway Went Thataway"

Fifth Wednesday online: "Leviticus"

Fledgling Rag: "Dear America," "Dear White [For decades]," "Even the Space," "We Are the World," and "W[h]it[e]tness"

Flyway: "Photo Negative: Sea"

Gargoyle: "We Thought We Were" and "Snow White"

Maryland Literary Review: "Wrack"

Mid-American Review: "Four and Twenty," "Rapunzel," and "The Pea"

National Poetry Review: "Spotting the Whale"

New South online: "The Rest of Her"

North American Review: "Big Hair"

Northern Virginia Review: "Phantoms," "Bad Parenting," and "Still Sea"

Passages North online: "Generosity"

Poet Lore: "Power: A Brief History" (as "Dear White") and "Southern Gothic"

Potomac Review: "There Is Only Now"

The Southern Review: "Genesis"

SLAB Litmag: "Rage"

Sugar House Review: "In the Past, the Present is the Future"

This is What America Looks Like: Poetry and Fiction from D.C., Maryland, and Virginia: "Dear White Girl" and "Southern Living"

Tusculum Review: "History"

Thank you to the Academy of American Poets for the Poet Laureate Fellowship that allowed me to pursue my work with young poets and gave me the time and space to complete this manuscript. Thanks also to the Virginia Center for the Creative Arts, where some of that work took place.

Thank you to Marymount University for the sabbatical and faculty development funds that helped support this manuscript at various stages.

Thank you to my friends and fellow poets who offered their feedback on this manuscript: Naomi Ayala, Brandel France de Bravo, Sid Gold, Robert Herschbach, Susan Mockler, Kirsten Porter and Sarah Trembath.

Thank you to the wonderful folks at Gunpowder Press for believing in this book and for their generous work in seeing it to print. Small independent presses are the backbone of American literature. Their work is woefully underfunded and absolutely invaluable.

Most importantly, thank you to my family—my parents, my husband, and my children. This book wouldn't exist without your love and support.

About the Poet

Holly Karapetkova is Poet Laureate Emerita of Arlington, Virginia, and a recipient of a 2022 Academy of American Poets Laureate Fellowship for her work with young poets. Her poetry, prose, and translations have appeared widely in print and online. She is the author of two books of poetry, *Towline*, winner of the Vern Rutsala Poetry Prize from Cloudbank Books, and *Words We Might One Day Say*, winner of the Washington Writers' Publishing House Prize for Poetry. She lives in Arlington, Virginia, and teaches at Marymount University.

ALSO FROM

GUNPOWDER PRESS

Learning to Drown, poems by SM Stubbs
Empty Me Full, poems by Catherine Abbey Hodges
Frangible Operas, poems by Susan Kelly-DeWitt
Before Traveling to Alabama, poems by David Case
Mother Lode, poems by Peg Quinn
Raft of Days, poems by Catherine Abbey Hodges
Unfinished City, poems by Nan Cohen
Original Face, poems by Jim Peterson
Shaping Water, poems by Barry Spacks
The Tarnation of Faust, poems by David Case
Mouth & Fruit, poems by Chryss Yost

CALIFORNIA POETS SERIES

In Praise of Late Wonder, poems by Lee Herrick
Downtime, poems by Gary Soto
Speech Crush, poems by Sandra McPherson
Our Music, poems by Dennis Schmitz
Gatherer's Alphabet, poems by Susan Kelly-DeWitt

DRYDEN-VREELAND BOOK PRIZE

Three-Day Weekend, poems by Christopher Blackman

BARRY SPACKS POETRY PRIZE

Dear Empire, poems by Holly Karapetkova
Burial Fragments, poems by Keith Ekiss
In the Cathedral of My Undoing, poems by Kellam Ayres
Accidental Garden, poems by Catherine Esposito Prescott
Like All Light, poems by Todd Copeland
Curriculum, poems by Meghan Dunn
Drinking with O'Hara, poems by Glenn Freeman
The Ghosts of Lost Animals, poems by Michelle Bonczek Evory
Posthumous Noon, poems by Aaron Baker
Burning Down Disneyland, poems by Kurt Olsson
Instead of Sadness, poems by Catherine Abbey Hodges

ALTA CALIFORNIA CHAPBOOKS

Alba and Other Songs, poems by Fred Arroyo
The First Amelia, poems by Amelia Rodriguez
On Display, poems by Gabriel Ibarra
Sor Juana, poems by Florencia Milito
Levitations, poems by Nicholas Reiner
Grief Logic, poems by Crystal AC Salas

FULL CATALOG AT GUNPOWDERPRESS.COM